FRIENDSHIP BREADS

Starters and Recipes

Compiled By
Jackie Gannaway

Published in Austin, TX by COOKBOOK CUPBOARD,
P.O. Box 50053, Austin, TX 78763 (512) 477-7070

ISBN 0-9629408-4-4

Artwork by Penny Graham
232 Gatewood Circle East Burleson, Texas 76028

Mail Order Information

There are three books on Friendship Breads in The Kitchen Crafts Collection. The first book is this book, "Friendship Breads, Starters and Recipes", the second is "Fat Free Friendship Breads, Starters and Recipes", thethird is "Fruit Friendship Breads, Starters and Recipes. There are many other fun titles in The Kitchen Crafts Collection. For a descriptive listing of all titles, send a note asking for an order blank.

To order one of the Friendship Breads books send a note telling which book(s) you want. Be very specific since the names of all three are so similar. They cost $3.95 each. TX residents add 8 % sales tax. Add $1.50 per order for shipping. Orders sent by Post Office and take 1 to 2 weeks to receive. For UPS shipping add $1.50 more and specify UPS.

Send to Cookbook Cupboard, P.O. Box 50053, Austin, TX 78763.

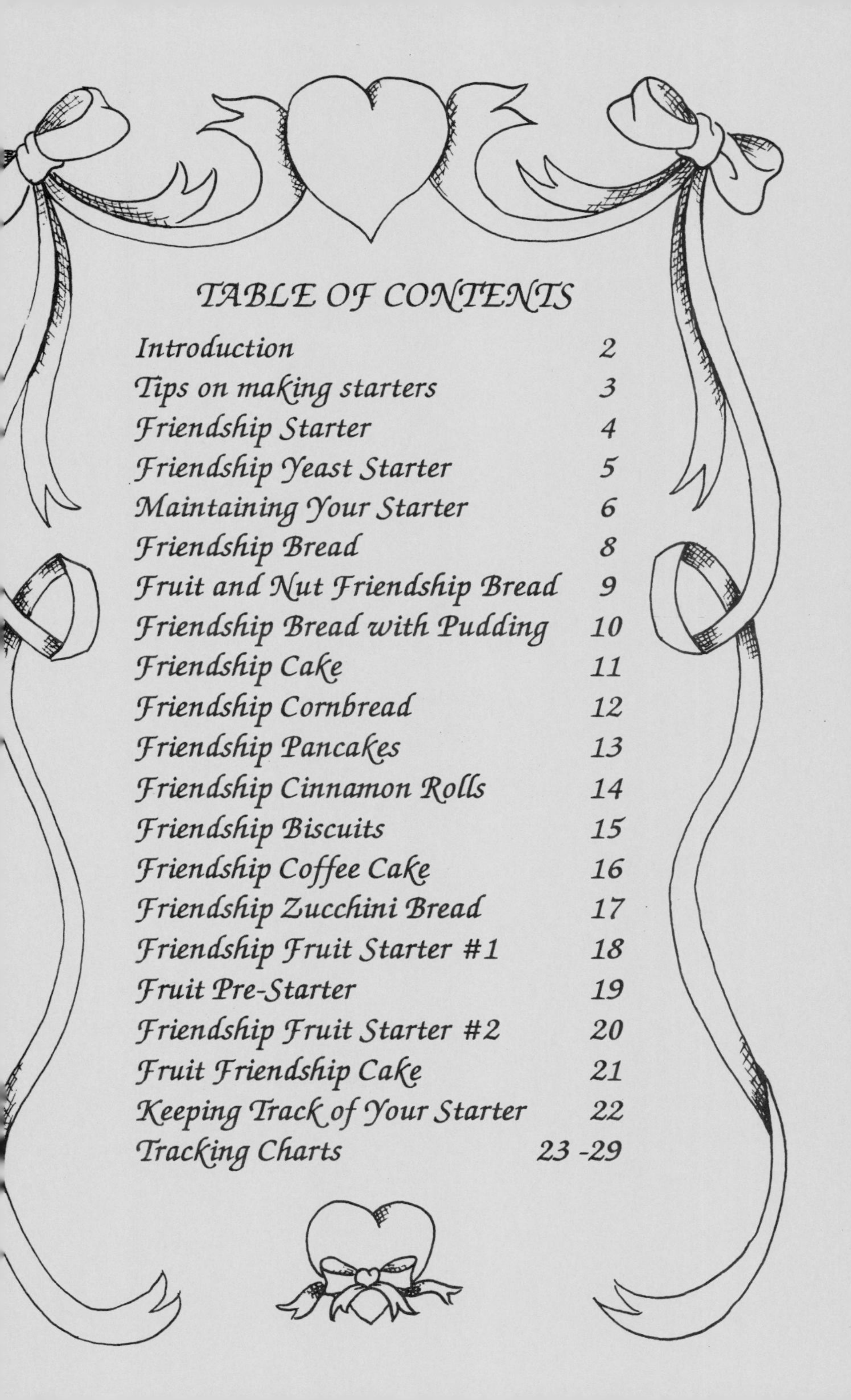

TABLE OF CONTENTS

Introduction 2
Tips on making starters 3
Friendship Starter 4
Friendship Yeast Starter 5
Maintaining Your Starter 6
Friendship Bread 8
Fruit and Nut Friendship Bread 9
Friendship Bread with Pudding 10
Friendship Cake 11
Friendship Cornbread 12
Friendship Pancakes 13
Friendship Cinnamon Rolls 14
Friendship Biscuits 15
Friendship Coffee Cake 16
Friendship Zucchini Bread 17
Friendship Fruit Starter #1 18
Fruit Pre-Starter 19
Friendship Fruit Starter #2 20
Fruit Friendship Cake 21
Keeping Track of Your Starter 22
Tracking Charts 23 -29

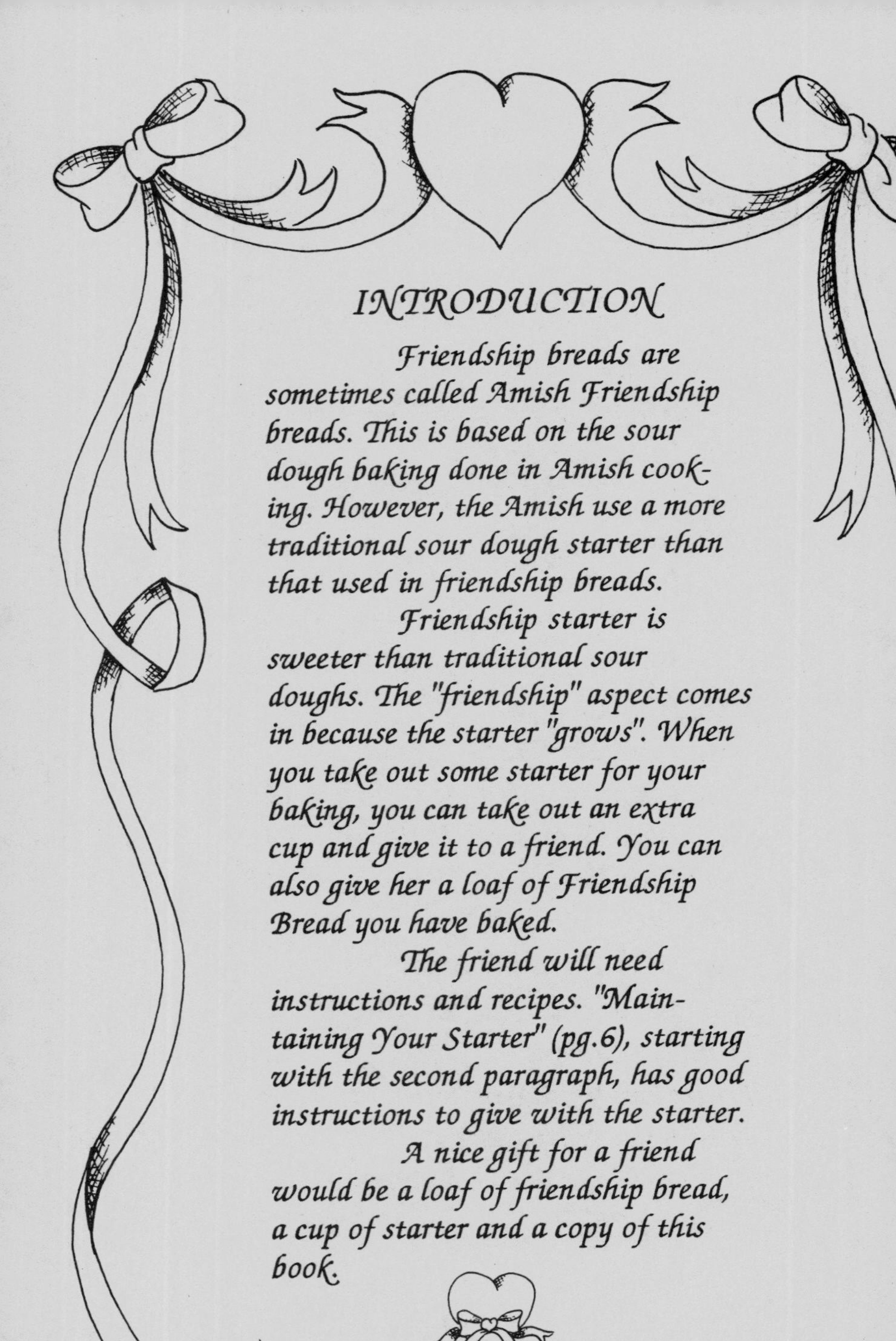

INTRODUCTION

Friendship breads are sometimes called Amish Friendship breads. This is based on the sour dough baking done in Amish cooking. However, the Amish use a more traditional sour dough starter than that used in friendship breads.

Friendship starter is sweeter than traditional sour doughs. The "friendship" aspect comes in because the starter "grows". When you take out some starter for your baking, you can take out an extra cup and give it to a friend. You can also give her a loaf of Friendship Bread you have baked.

The friend will need instructions and recipes. "Maintaining Your Starter" (pg.6), starting with the second paragraph, has good instructions to give with the starter.

A nice gift for a friend would be a loaf of friendship bread, a cup of starter and a copy of this book.

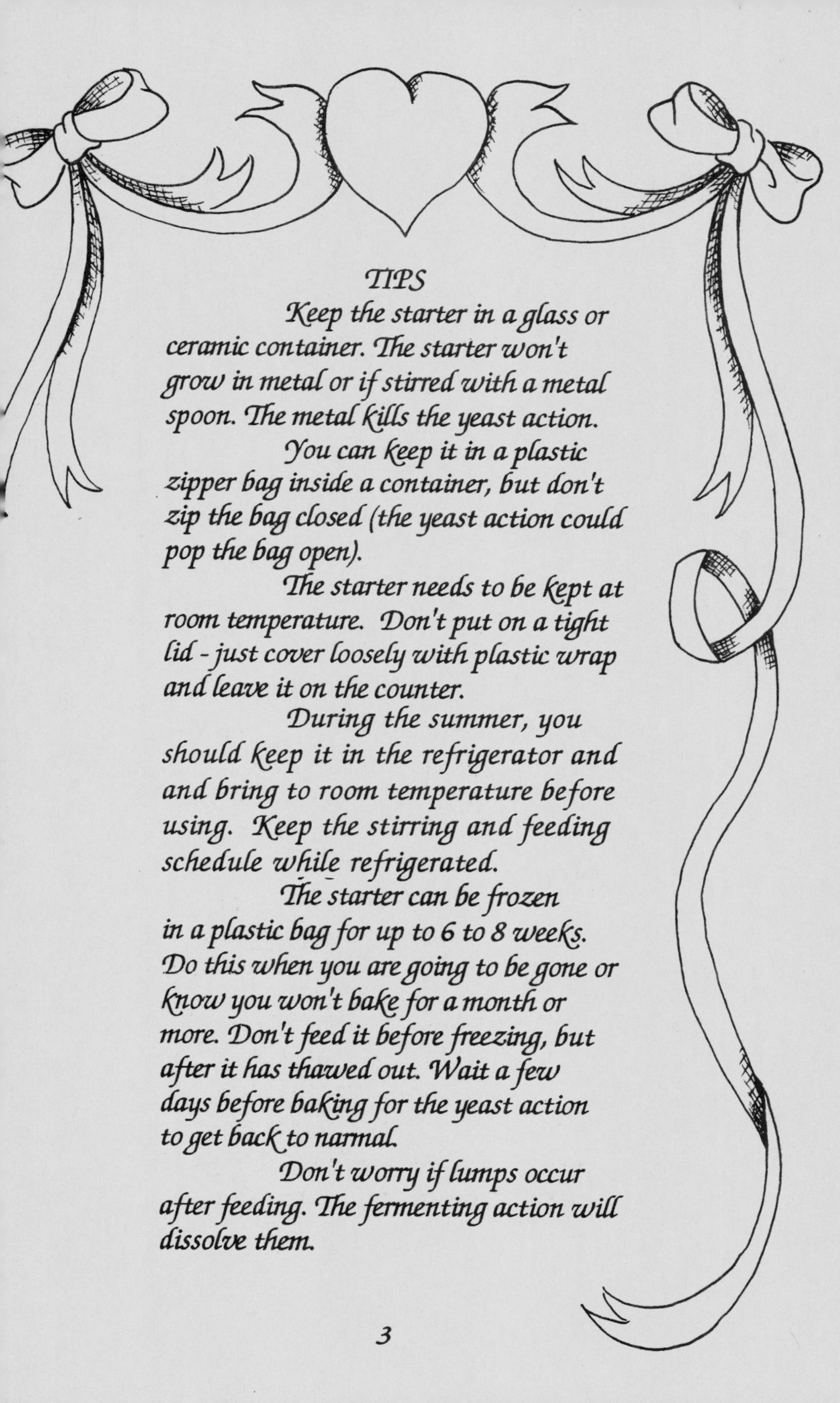

TIPS

Keep the starter in a glass or ceramic container. The starter won't grow in metal or if stirred with a metal spoon. The metal kills the yeast action.

You can keep it in a plastic zipper bag inside a container, but don't zip the bag closed (the yeast action could pop the bag open).

The starter needs to be kept at room temperature. Don't put on a tight lid - just cover loosely with plastic wrap and leave it on the counter.

During the summer, you should keep it in the refrigerator and and bring to room temperature before using. Keep the stirring and feeding schedule while refrigerated.

The starter can be frozen in a plastic bag for up to 6 to 8 weeks. Do this when you are going to be gone or know you won't bake for a month or more. Don't feed it before freezing, but after it has thawed out. Wait a few days before baking for the yeast action to get back to narmal.

Don't worry if lumps occur after feeding. The fermenting action will dissolve them.

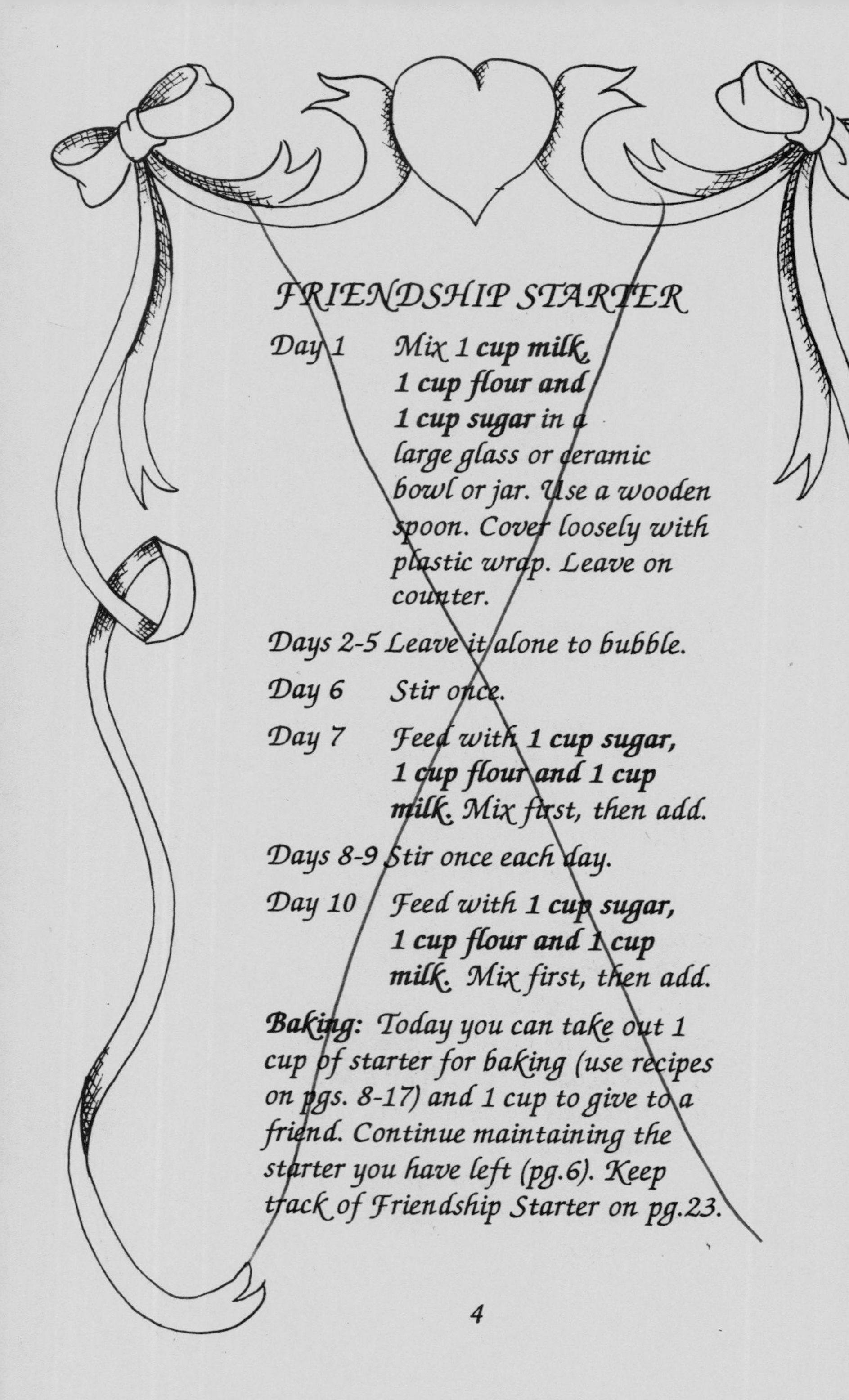

FRIENDSHIP STARTER

Day 1 — Mix **1 cup milk, 1 cup flour and 1 cup sugar** in a large glass or ceramic bowl or jar. Use a wooden spoon. Cover loosely with plastic wrap. Leave on counter.

Days 2-5 — Leave it alone to bubble.

Day 6 — Stir once.

Day 7 — Feed with **1 cup sugar, 1 cup flour and 1 cup milk.** Mix first, then add.

Days 8-9 — Stir once each day.

Day 10 — Feed with **1 cup sugar, 1 cup flour and 1 cup milk.** Mix first, then add.

Baking: Today you can take out 1 cup of starter for baking (use recipes on pgs. 8-17) and 1 cup to give to a friend. Continue maintaining the starter you have left (pg.6). Keep track of Friendship Starter on pg.23.

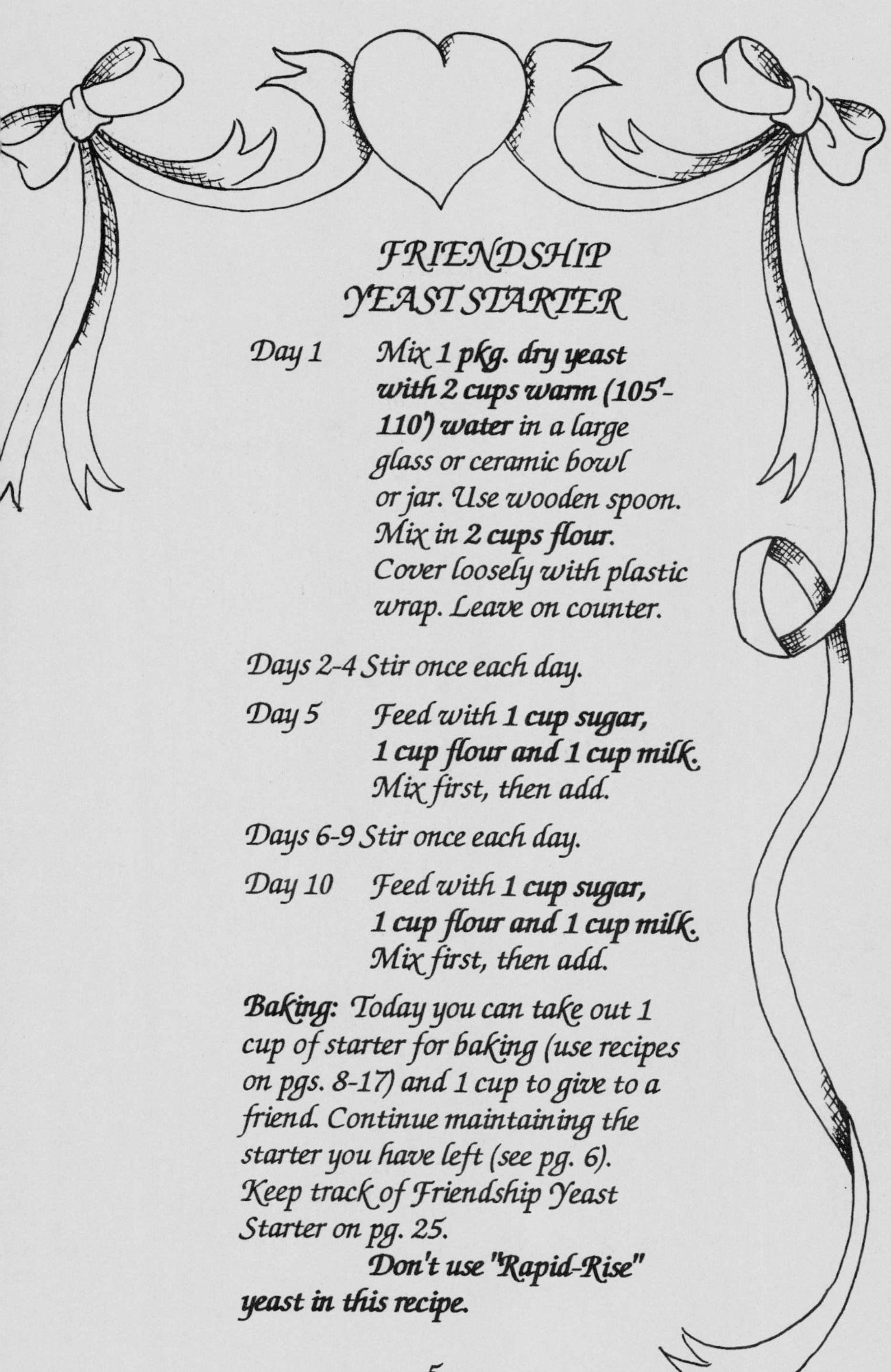

FRIENDSHIP YEAST STARTER

Day 1 — Mix **1 pkg. dry yeast with 2 cups warm (105'-110') water** in a large glass or ceramic bowl or jar. Use wooden spoon. Mix in **2 cups flour**. Cover loosely with plastic wrap. Leave on counter.

Days 2-4 Stir once each day.

Day 5 — Feed with **1 cup sugar, 1 cup flour and 1 cup milk.** Mix first, then add.

Days 6-9 Stir once each day.

Day 10 — Feed with **1 cup sugar, 1 cup flour and 1 cup milk.** Mix first, then add.

Baking: Today you can take out 1 cup of starter for baking (use recipes on pgs. 8-17) and 1 cup to give to a friend. Continue maintaining the starter you have left (see pg. 6). Keep track of Friendship Yeast Starter on pg. 25.

Don't use "Rapid-Rise" yeast in this recipe.

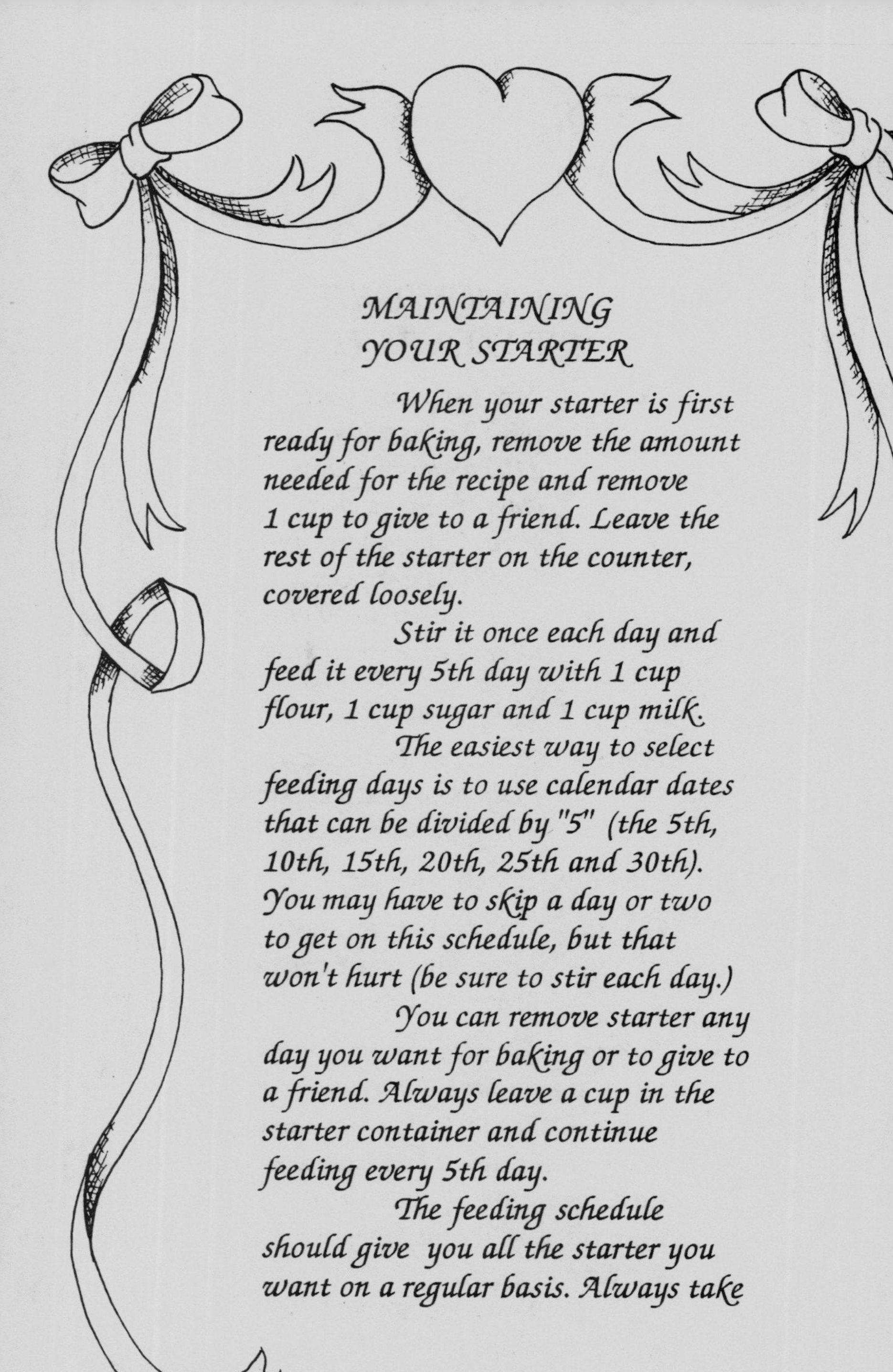

MAINTAINING YOUR STARTER

When your starter is first ready for baking, remove the amount needed for the recipe and remove 1 cup to give to a friend. Leave the rest of the starter on the counter, covered loosely.

Stir it once each day and feed it every 5th day with 1 cup flour, 1 cup sugar and 1 cup milk.

The easiest way to select feeding days is to use calendar dates that can be divided by "5" (the 5th, 10th, 15th, 20th, 25th and 30th). You may have to skip a day or two to get on this schedule, but that won't hurt (be sure to stir each day.)

You can remove starter any day you want for baking or to give to a friend. Always leave a cup in the starter container and continue feeding every 5th day.

The feeding schedule should give you all the starter you want on a regular basis. Always take

out 1 or 2 cups after feeding. If you don't need any starter for baking or giving, you will still have to take some out and discard it. This way you will always have a manageable amount of fresh starter.

Every 30 days, transfer your starter to another container and thoroughly wash and scald the container before putting the starter back in. If your starter is in a plastic bag, change bags every 30 days.

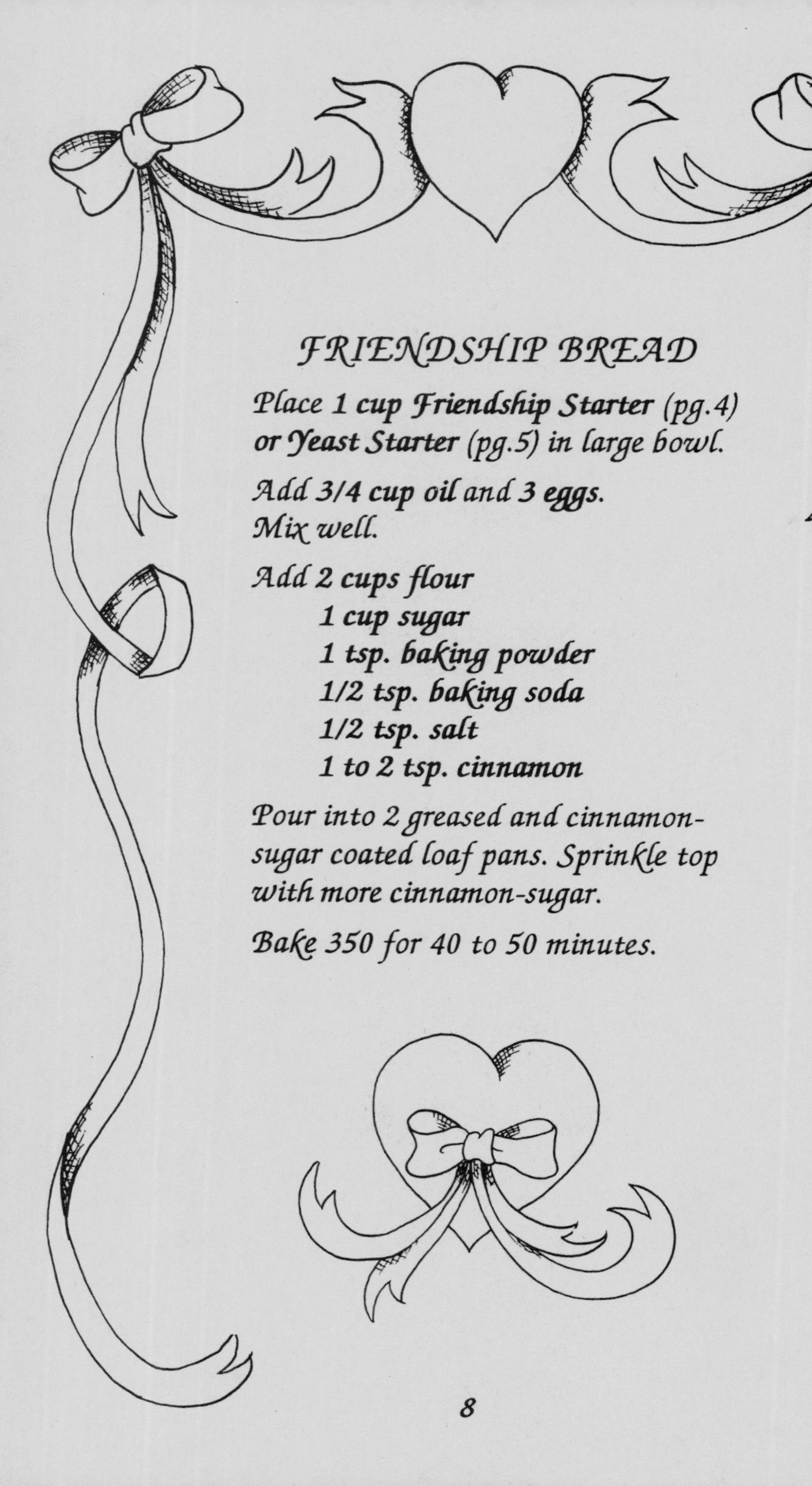

FRIENDSHIP BREAD

Place **1 cup Friendship Starter** (pg.4) or **Yeast Starter** (pg.5) in large bowl.

Add **3/4 cup oil** and **3 eggs.**
Mix well.

Add **2 cups flour**
1 cup sugar
1 tsp. baking powder
1/2 tsp. baking soda
1/2 tsp. salt
1 to 2 tsp. cinnamon

Pour into 2 greased and cinnamon-sugar coated loaf pans. Sprinkle top with more cinnamon-sugar.

Bake 350 for 40 to 50 minutes.

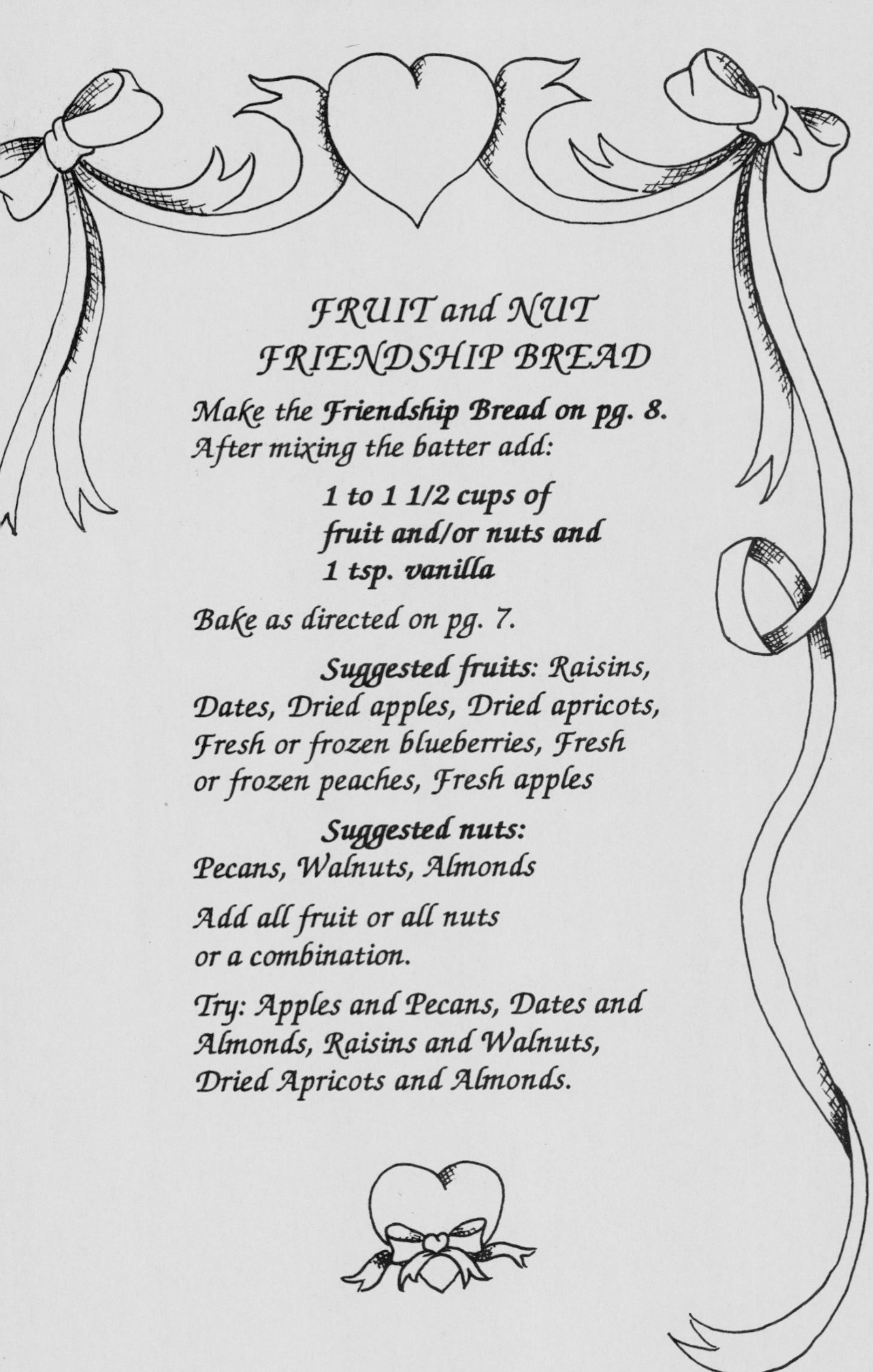

FRUIT and NUT FRIENDSHIP BREAD

Make the **Friendship Bread on pg. 8.**
After mixing the batter add:

1 to 1 1/2 cups of
fruit and/or nuts and
1 tsp. vanilla

Bake as directed on pg. 7.

Suggested fruits: Raisins, Dates, Dried apples, Dried apricots, Fresh or frozen blueberries, Fresh or frozen peaches, Fresh apples

Suggested nuts:
Pecans, Walnuts, Almonds

Add all fruit or all nuts or a combination.

Try: Apples and Pecans, Dates and Almonds, Raisins and Walnuts, Dried Apricots and Almonds.

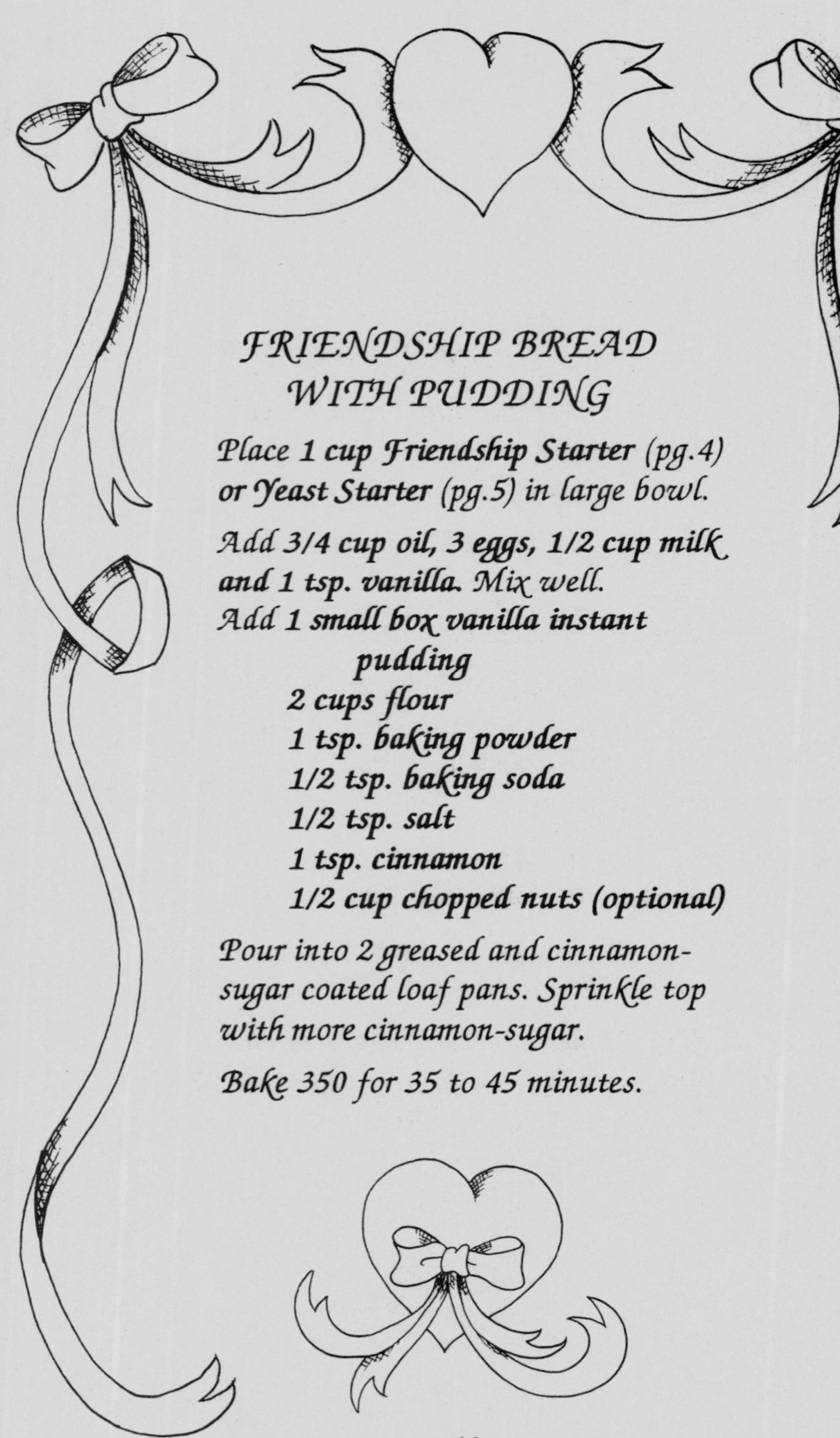

FRIENDSHIP BREAD WITH PUDDING

Place 1 cup Friendship Starter (pg.4) or Yeast Starter (pg.5) in large bowl.

Add 3/4 cup oil, 3 eggs, 1/2 cup milk and 1 tsp. vanilla. Mix well.

Add 1 small box vanilla instant pudding
2 cups flour
1 tsp. baking powder
1/2 tsp. baking soda
1/2 tsp. salt
1 tsp. cinnamon
1/2 cup chopped nuts (optional)

Pour into 2 greased and cinnamon-sugar coated loaf pans. Sprinkle top with more cinnamon-sugar.

Bake 350 for 35 to 45 minutes.

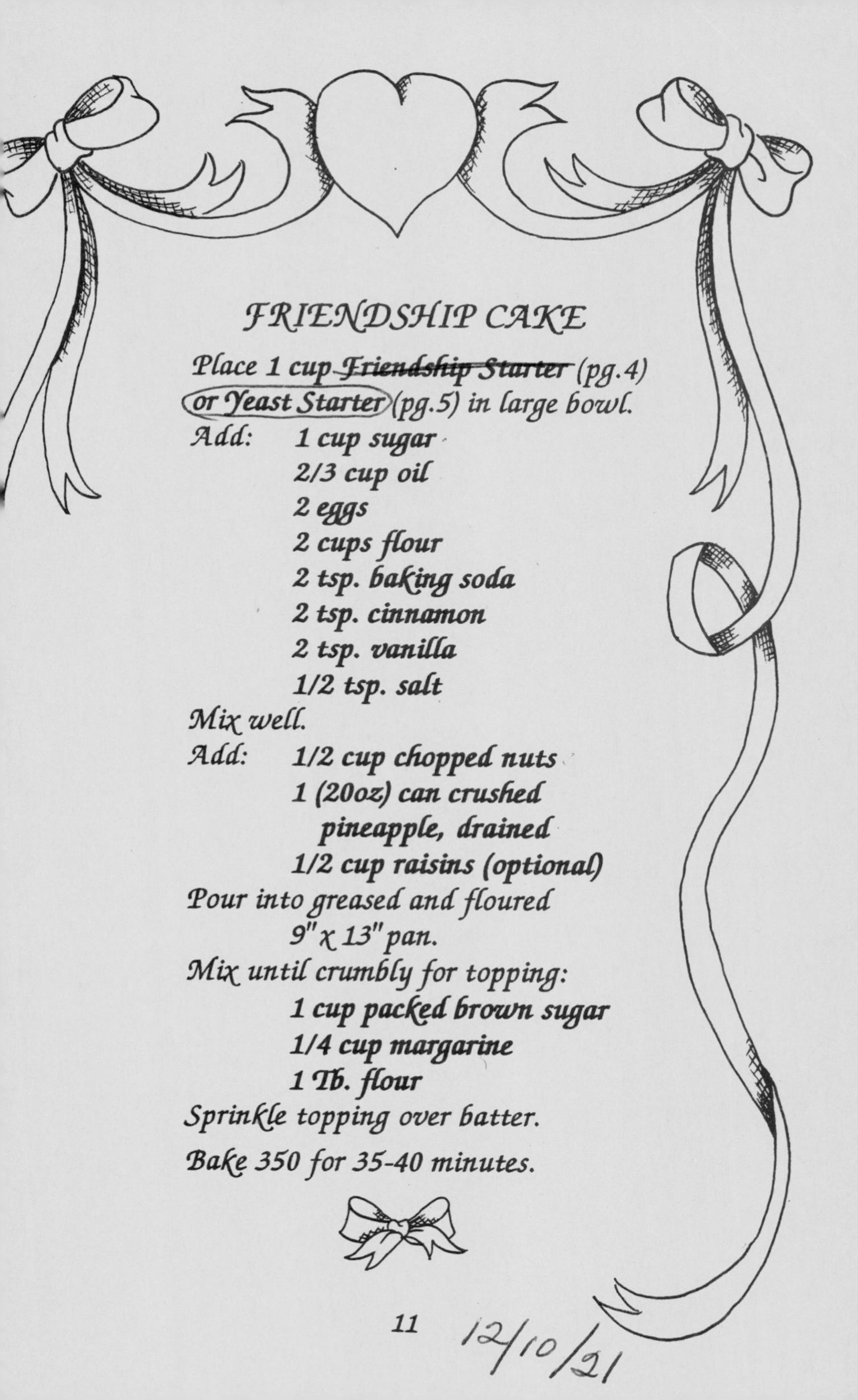

FRIENDSHIP CAKE

Place 1 cup ~~Friendship Starter~~ (pg.4) or Yeast Starter (pg.5) in large bowl.

Add:
- 1 cup sugar
- 2/3 cup oil
- 2 eggs
- 2 cups flour
- 2 tsp. baking soda
- 2 tsp. cinnamon
- 2 tsp. vanilla
- 1/2 tsp. salt

Mix well.

Add:
- 1/2 cup chopped nuts
- 1 (20oz) can crushed pineapple, drained
- 1/2 cup raisins (optional)

Pour into greased and floured 9" x 13" pan.

Mix until crumbly for topping:
- 1 cup packed brown sugar
- 1/4 cup margarine
- 1 Tb. flour

Sprinkle topping over batter.

Bake 350 for 35-40 minutes.

12/10/21

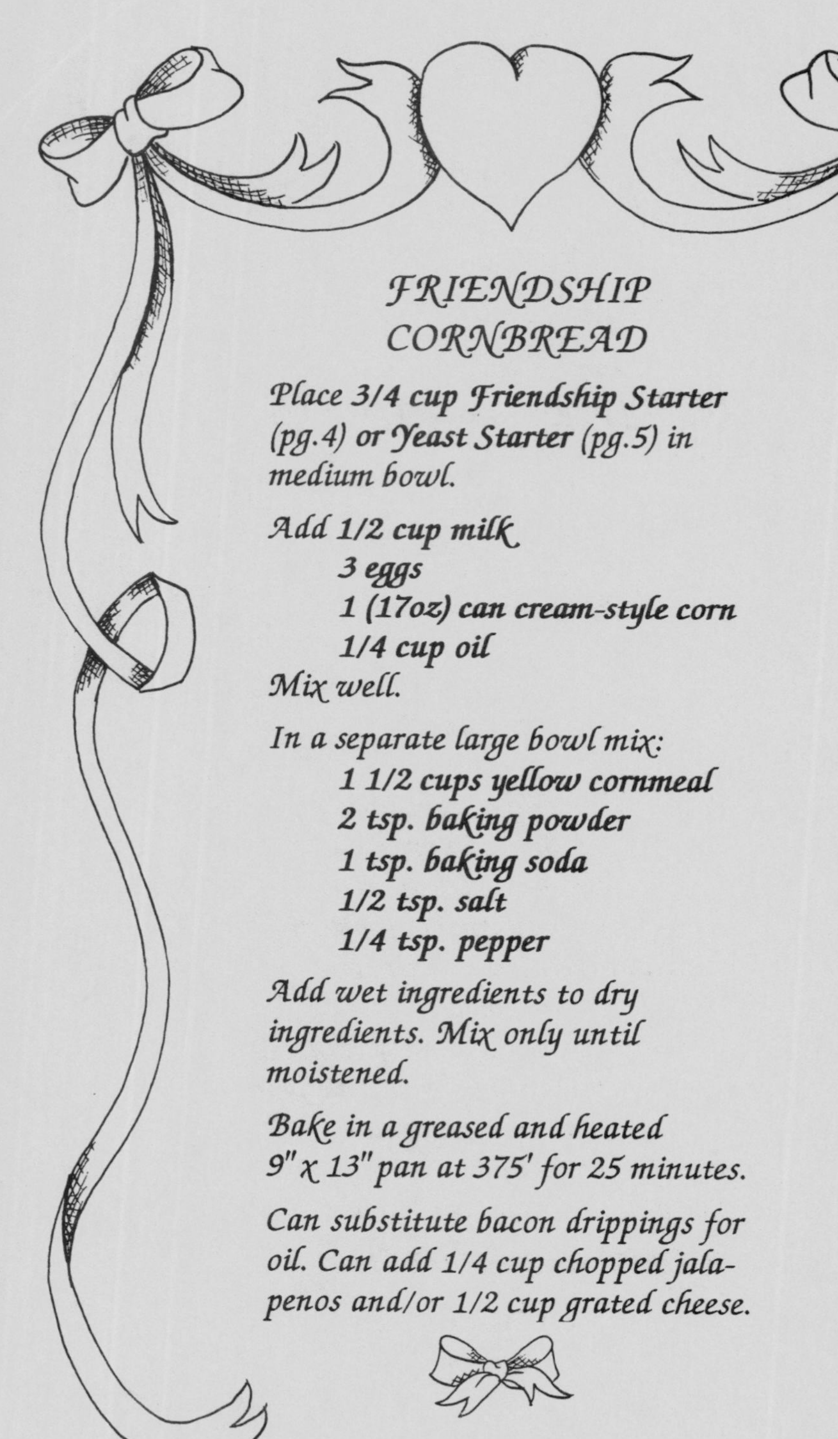

FRIENDSHIP CORNBREAD

Place 3/4 cup Friendship Starter (pg.4) or Yeast Starter (pg.5) in medium bowl.

Add 1/2 cup milk
3 eggs
1 (17oz) can cream-style corn
1/4 cup oil

Mix well.

In a separate large bowl mix:
1 1/2 cups yellow cornmeal
2 tsp. baking powder
1 tsp. baking soda
1/2 tsp. salt
1/4 tsp. pepper

Add wet ingredients to dry ingredients. Mix only until moistened.

Bake in a greased and heated 9" x 13" pan at 375' for 25 minutes.

Can substitute bacon drippings for oil. Can add 1/4 cup chopped jalapenos and/or 1/2 cup grated cheese.

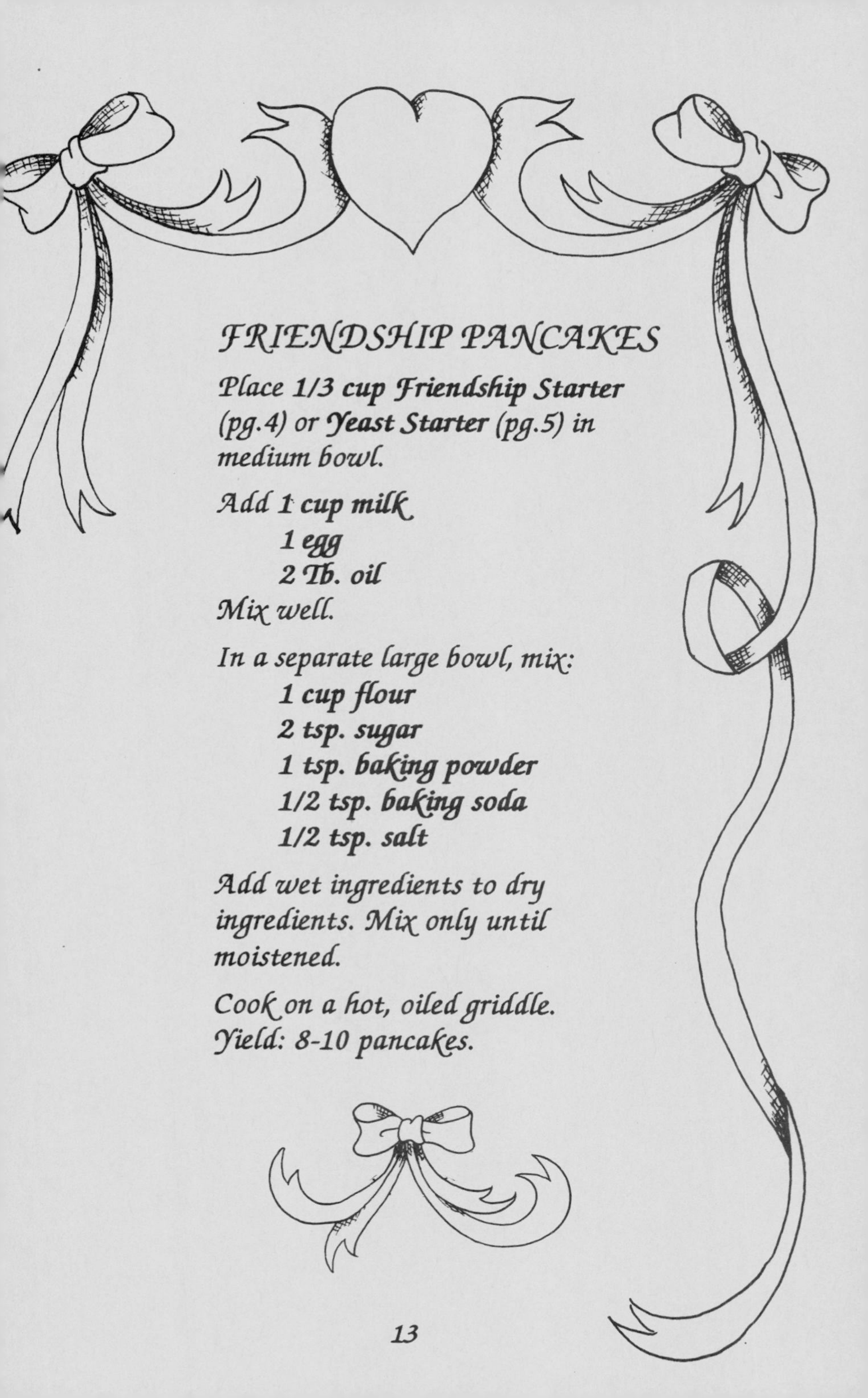

FRIENDSHIP PANCAKES

*Place **1/3 cup Friendship Starter** (pg.4) or **Yeast Starter** (pg.5) in medium bowl.*

*Add **1 cup milk***
1 egg
2 Tb. oil
Mix well.

In a separate large bowl, mix:
1 cup flour
2 tsp. sugar
1 tsp. baking powder
1/2 tsp. baking soda
1/2 tsp. salt

Add wet ingredients to dry ingredients. Mix only until moistened.

Cook on a hot, oiled griddle.
Yield: 8-10 pancakes.

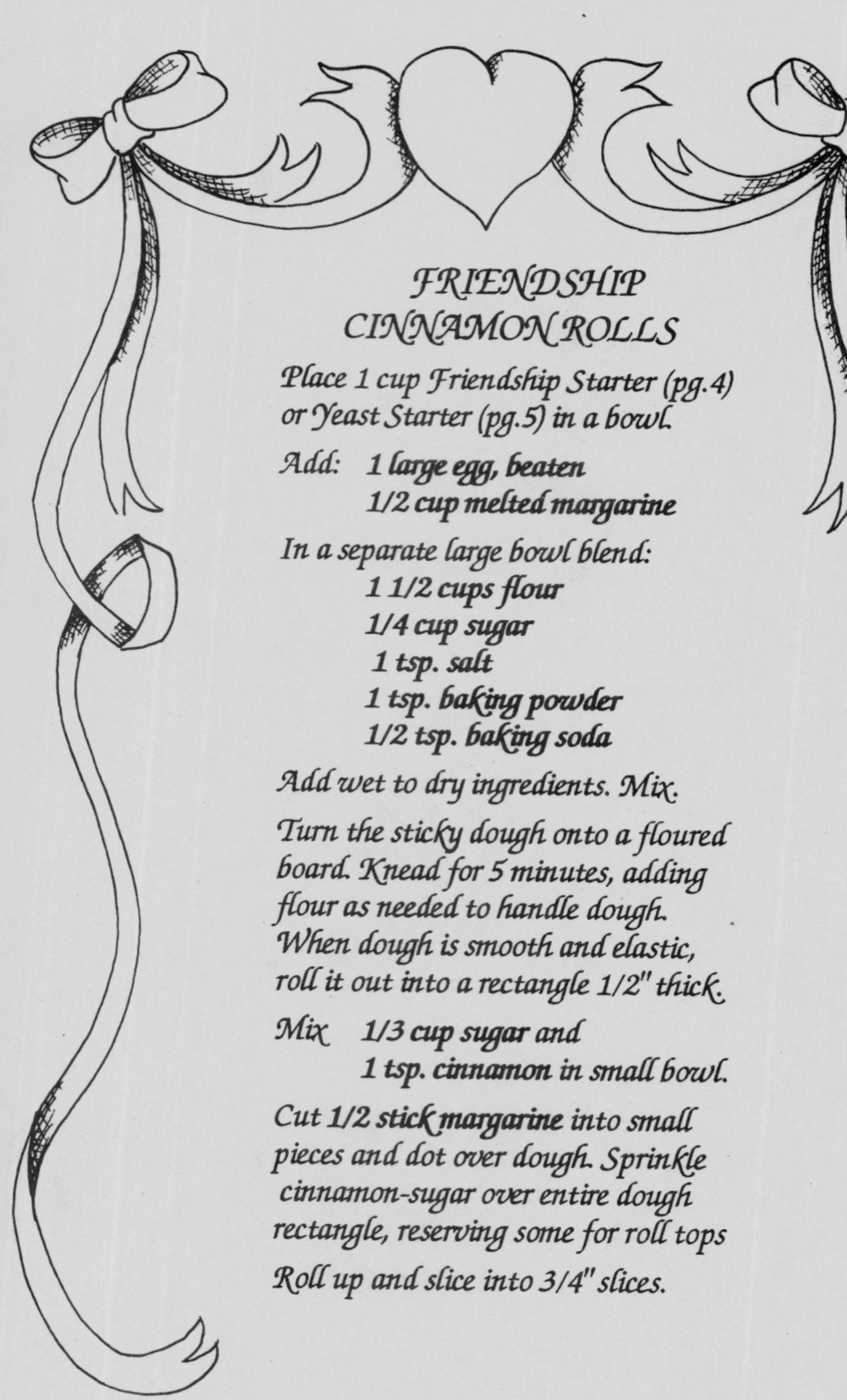

FRIENDSHIP CINNAMON ROLLS

Place 1 cup Friendship Starter (pg.4) or Yeast Starter (pg.5) in a bowl.

Add: **1 large egg, beaten**
1/2 cup melted margarine

In a separate large bowl blend:
1 1/2 cups flour
1/4 cup sugar
1 tsp. salt
1 tsp. baking powder
1/2 tsp. baking soda

Add wet to dry ingredients. Mix.

Turn the sticky dough onto a floured board. Knead for 5 minutes, adding flour as needed to handle dough. When dough is smooth and elastic, roll it out into a rectangle 1/2" thick.

Mix **1/3 cup sugar** and
1 tsp. cinnamon in small bowl.

Cut **1/2 stick margarine** into small pieces and dot over dough. Sprinkle cinnamon-sugar over entire dough rectangle, reserving some for roll tops

Roll up and slice into 3/4" slices.

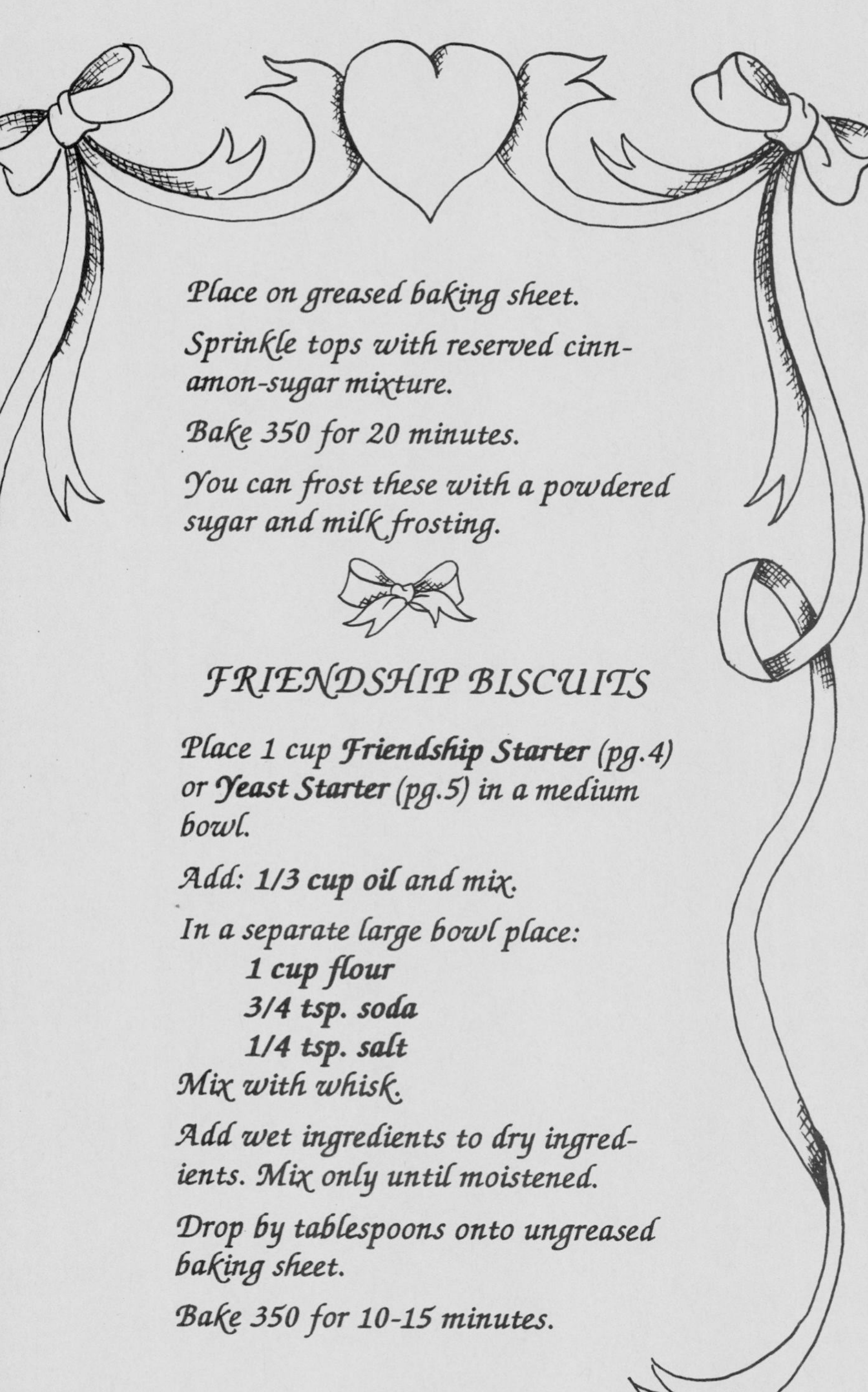

Place on greased baking sheet.

Sprinkle tops with reserved cinnamon-sugar mixture.

Bake 350 for 20 minutes.

You can frost these with a powdered sugar and milk frosting.

FRIENDSHIP BISCUITS

Place 1 cup **Friendship Starter** (pg.4) or **Yeast Starter** (pg.5) in a medium bowl.

Add: **1/3 cup oil** and mix.

In a separate large bowl place:

1 cup flour
3/4 tsp. soda
1/4 tsp. salt

Mix with whisk.

Add wet ingredients to dry ingredients. Mix only until moistened.

Drop by tablespoons onto ungreased baking sheet.

Bake 350 for 10-15 minutes.

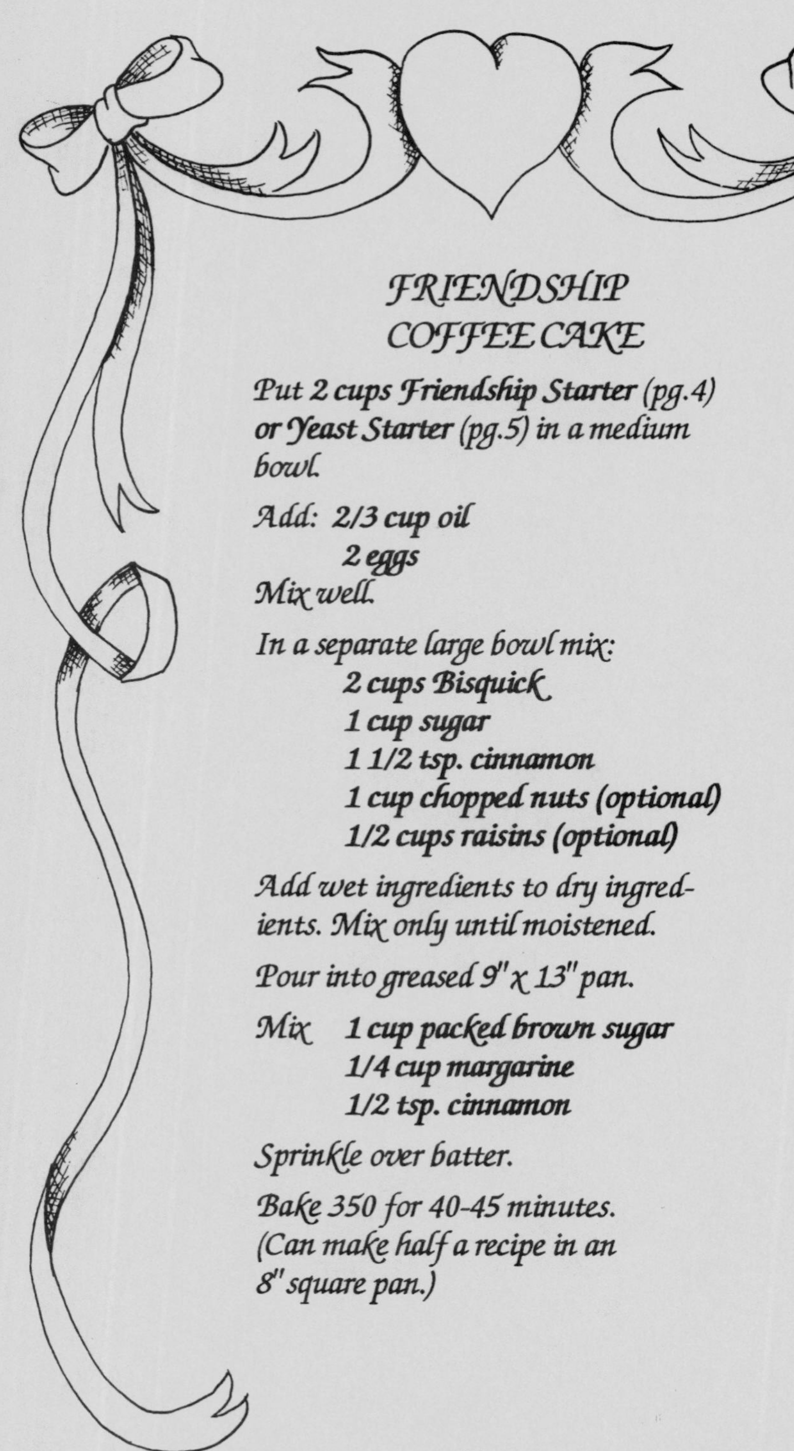

FRIENDSHIP COFFEE CAKE

Put 2 cups Friendship Starter (pg.4) or Yeast Starter (pg.5) in a medium bowl.

Add: 2/3 cup oil
2 eggs

Mix well.

In a separate large bowl mix:
2 cups Bisquick
1 cup sugar
1 1/2 tsp. cinnamon
1 cup chopped nuts (optional)
1/2 cups raisins (optional)

Add wet ingredients to dry ingredients. Mix only until moistened.

Pour into greased 9" x 13" pan.

Mix 1 cup packed brown sugar
1/4 cup margarine
1/2 tsp. cinnamon

Sprinkle over batter.

Bake 350 for 40-45 minutes. (Can make half a recipe in an 8" square pan.)

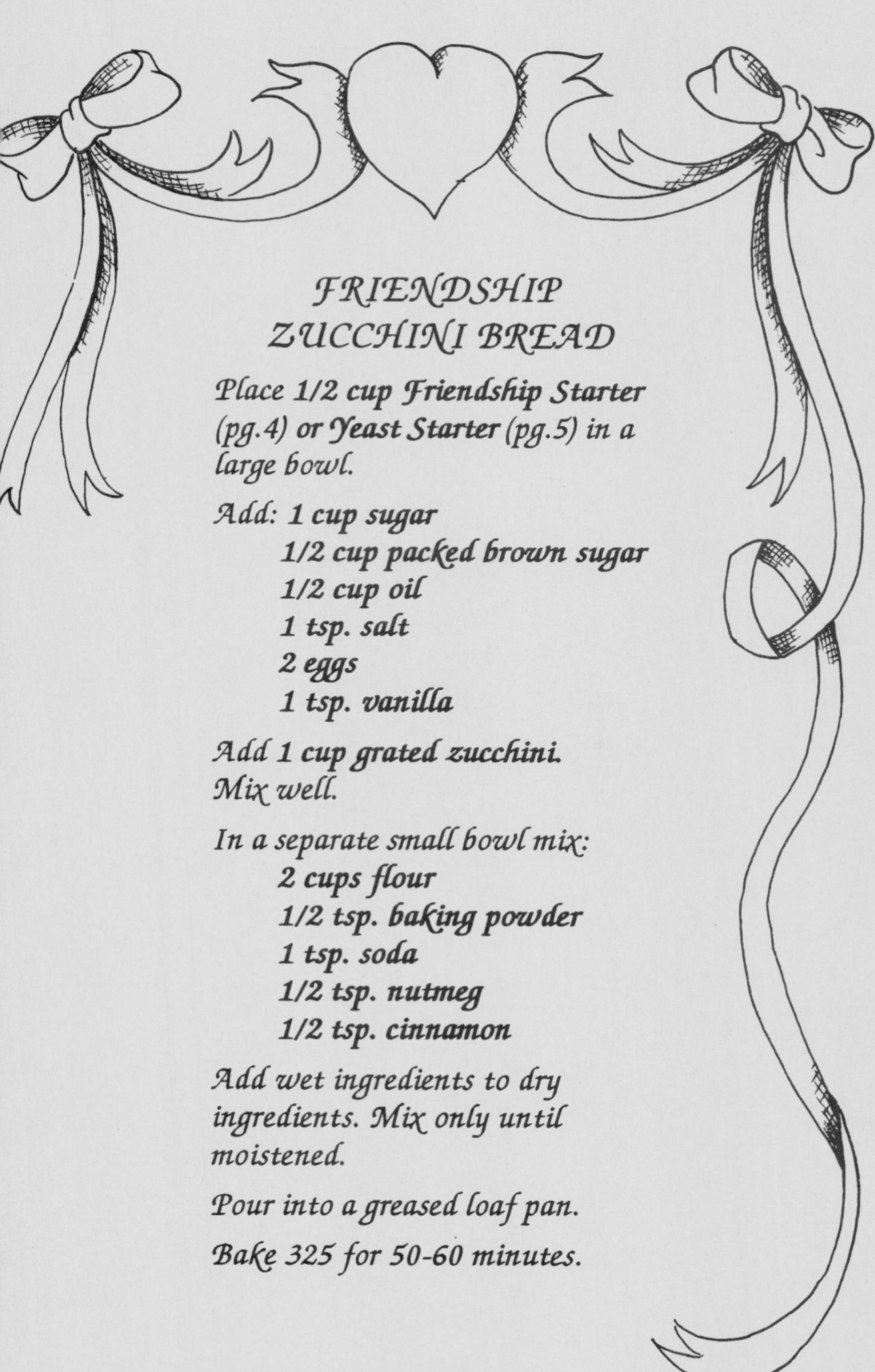

FRIENDSHIP ZUCCHINI BREAD

Place 1/2 cup Friendship Starter (pg.4) or Yeast Starter (pg.5) in a large bowl.

Add: 1 cup sugar
- 1/2 cup packed brown sugar
- 1/2 cup oil
- 1 tsp. salt
- 2 eggs
- 1 tsp. vanilla

Add 1 cup grated zucchini.
Mix well.

In a separate small bowl mix:
- 2 cups flour
- 1/2 tsp. baking powder
- 1 tsp. soda
- 1/2 tsp. nutmeg
- 1/2 tsp. cinnamon

Add wet ingredients to dry ingredients. Mix only until moistened.

Pour into a greased loaf pan.

Bake 325 for 50-60 minutes.

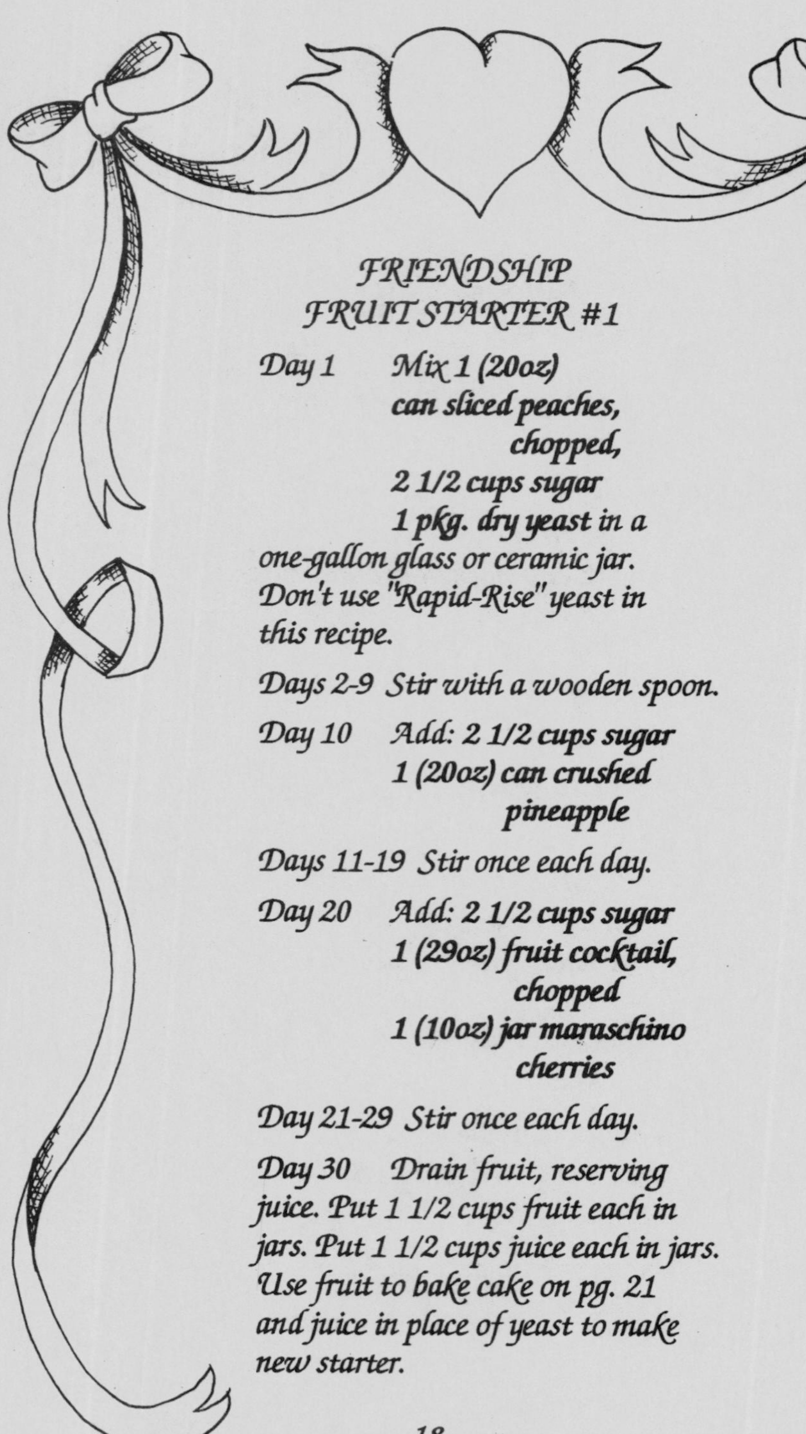

FRIENDSHIP FRUIT STARTER #1

Day 1 — Mix 1 (20oz) **can sliced peaches, chopped,**
2 1/2 cups sugar
1 pkg. dry yeast in a one-gallon glass or ceramic jar. Don't use "Rapid-Rise" yeast in this recipe.

Days 2-9 — Stir with a wooden spoon.

Day 10 — Add: **2 1/2 cups sugar**
1 (20oz) can crushed pineapple

Days 11-19 — Stir once each day.

Day 20 — Add: **2 1/2 cups sugar**
1 (29oz) fruit cocktail, chopped
1 (10oz) jar maraschino cherries

Day 21-29 — Stir once each day.

Day 30 — Drain fruit, reserving juice. Put 1 1/2 cups fruit each in jars. Put 1 1/2 cups juice each in jars. Use fruit to bake cake on pg. 21 and juice in place of yeast to make new starter.

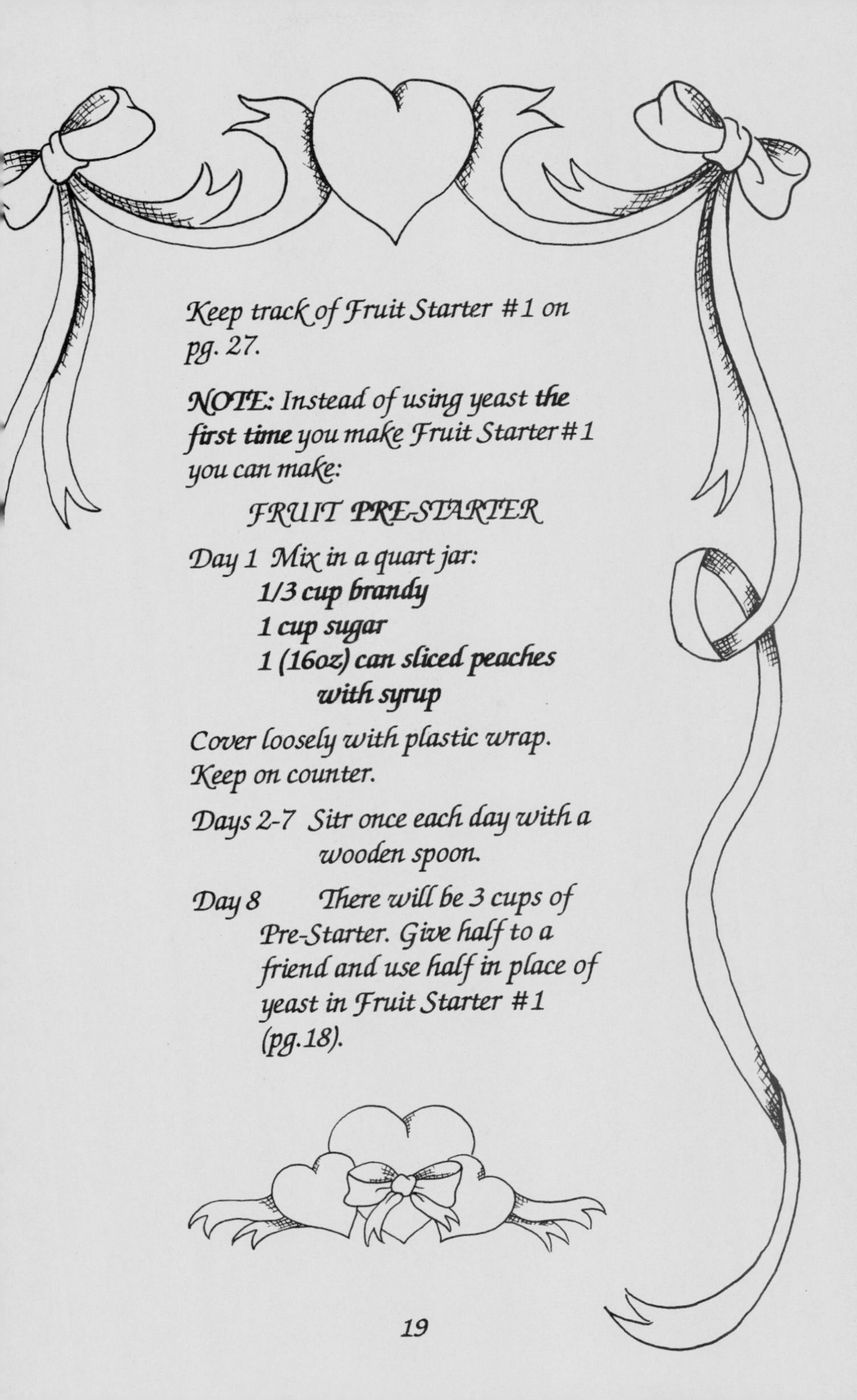

Keep track of Fruit Starter #1 on pg. 27.

***NOTE:** Instead of using yeast **the first time** you make Fruit Starter #1 you can make:*

FRUIT PRE-STARTER

Day 1 Mix in a quart jar:

1/3 cup brandy
1 cup sugar
1 (16oz) can sliced peaches with syrup

Cover loosely with plastic wrap. Keep on counter.

Days 2-7 Sitr once each day with a wooden spoon.

Day 8 There will be 3 cups of Pre-Starter. Give half to a friend and use half in place of yeast in Fruit Starter #1 (pg.18).

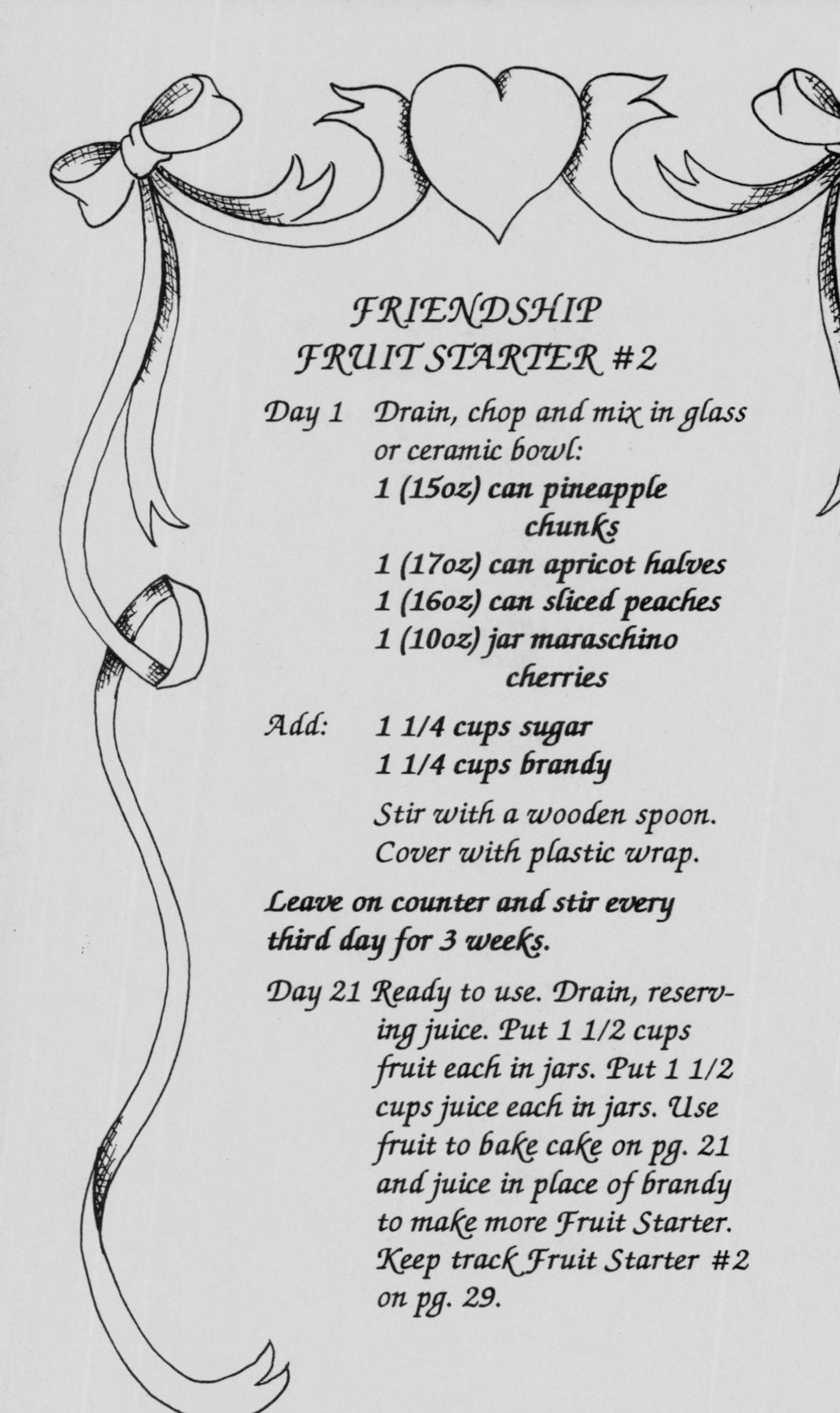

FRIENDSHIP FRUIT STARTER #2

Day 1 Drain, chop and mix in glass or ceramic bowl:

1 (15oz) can pineapple chunks
1 (17oz) can apricot halves
1 (16oz) can sliced peaches
1 (10oz) jar maraschino cherries

Add: **1 1/4 cups sugar**
1 1/4 cups brandy

Stir with a wooden spoon. Cover with plastic wrap.

Leave on counter and stir every third day for 3 weeks.

Day 21 Ready to use. Drain, reserving juice. Put 1 1/2 cups fruit each in jars. Put 1 1/2 cups juice each in jars. Use fruit to bake cake on pg. 21 and juice in place of brandy to make more Fruit Starter. Keep track Fruit Starter #2 on pg. 29.

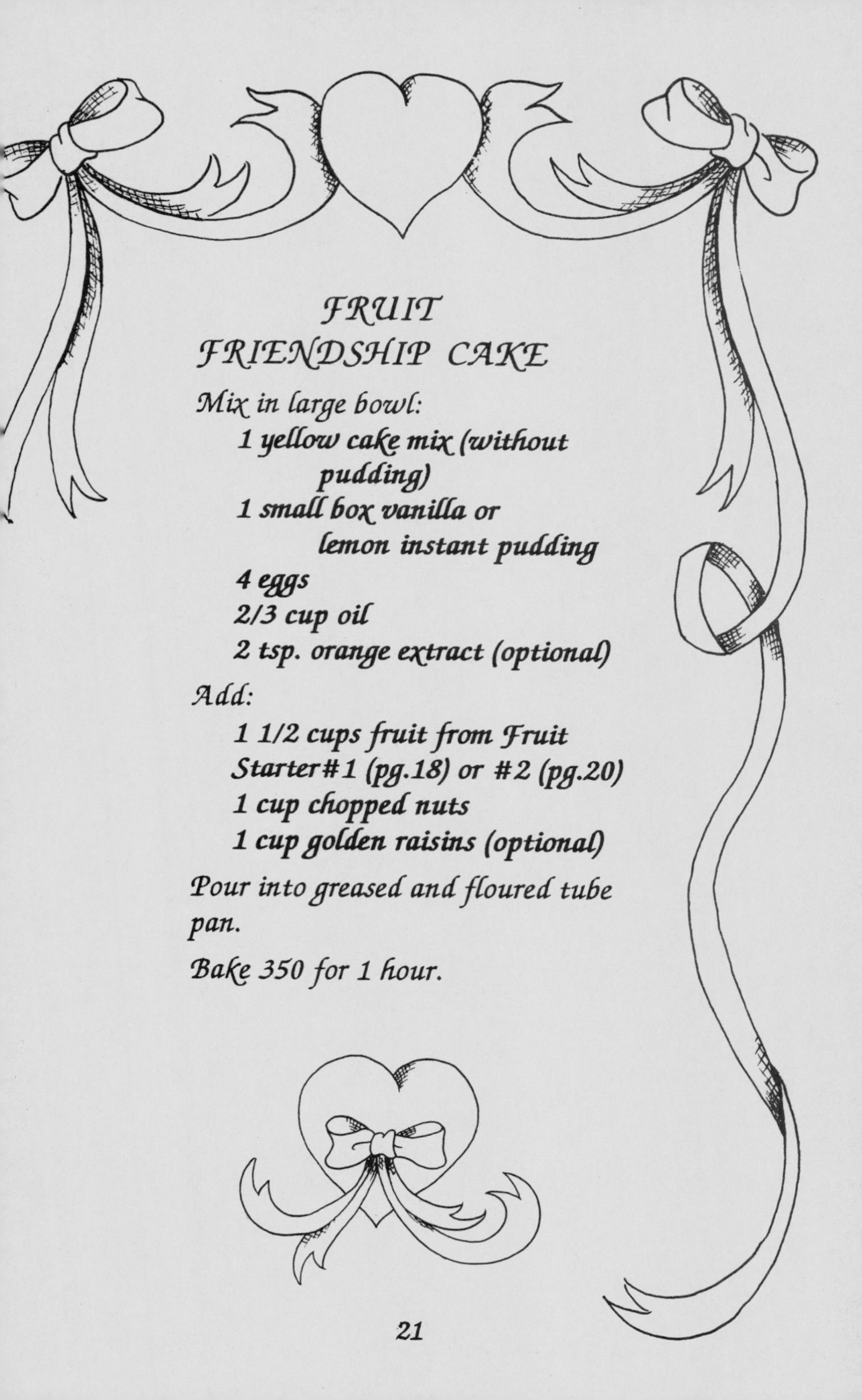

FRUIT FRIENDSHIP CAKE

Mix in large bowl:

1 yellow cake mix (without pudding)
1 small box vanilla or lemon instant pudding
4 eggs
2/3 cup oil
2 tsp. orange extract (optional)

Add:

1 1/2 cups fruit from Fruit Starter #1 (pg.18) or #2 (pg.20)
1 cup chopped nuts
1 cup golden raisins (optional)

Pour into greased and floured tube pan.

Bake 350 for 1 hour.

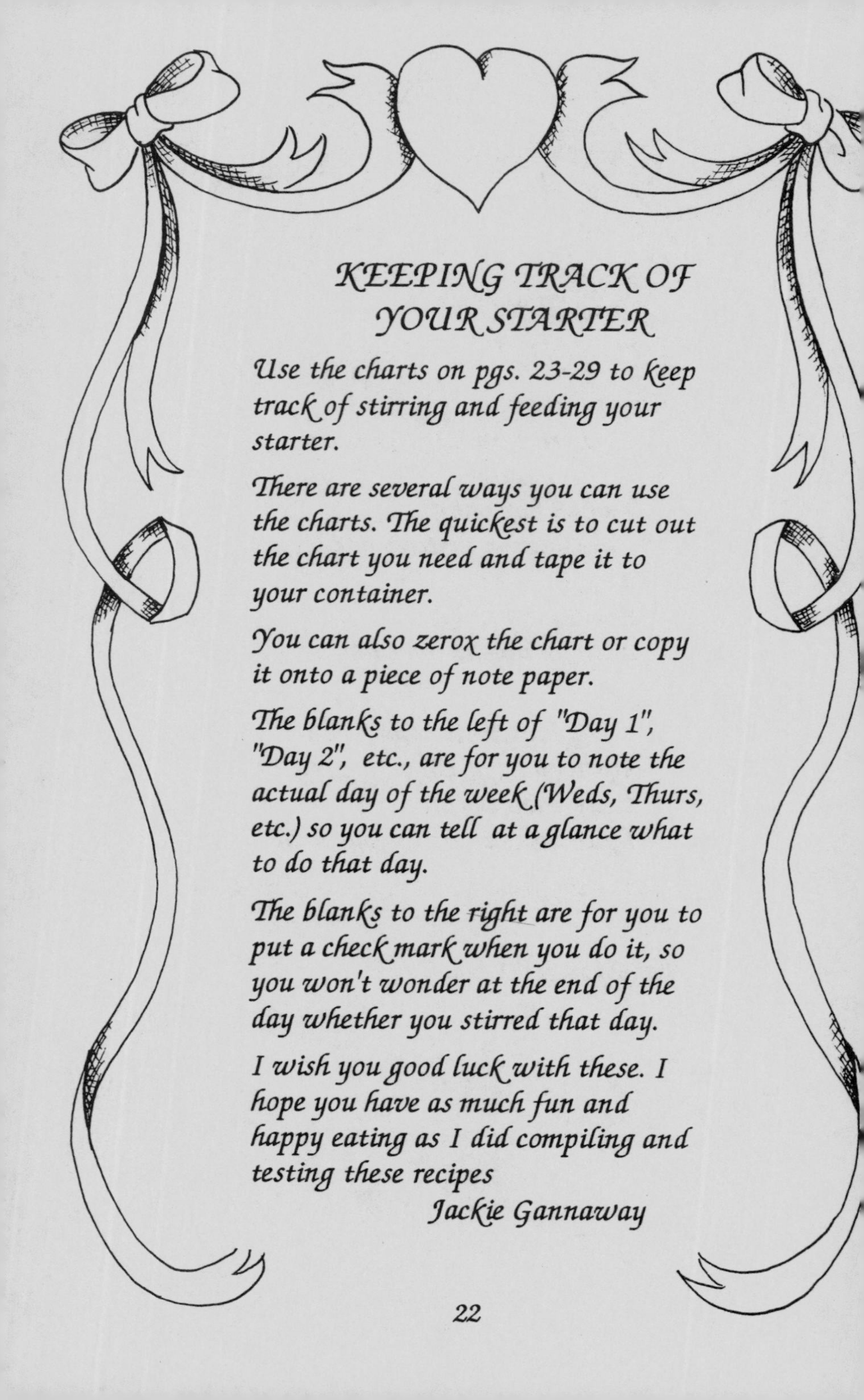

KEEPING TRACK OF YOUR STARTER

Use the charts on pgs. 23-29 to keep track of stirring and feeding your starter.

There are several ways you can use the charts. The quickest is to cut out the chart you need and tape it to your container.

You can also zerox the chart or copy it onto a piece of note paper.

The blanks to the left of "Day 1", "Day 2", etc., are for you to note the actual day of the week (Weds, Thurs, etc.) so you can tell at a glance what to do that day.

The blanks to the right are for you to put a check mark when you do it, so you won't wonder at the end of the day whether you stirred that day.

I wish you good luck with these. I hope you have as much fun and happy eating as I did compiling and testing these recipes

Jackie Gannaway

Keep track of

FRIENDSHIP STARTER (pg.4)

______	Day 1	Mix ingredients.
______	Days 2-5	Leave alone.
______	Day 6	Stir one time. ______
______	Day 7	Feed. ______
______	Day 8	Stir one time. ______
______	Day 9	Stir one time. ______
______	Day 10	Feed. ______
		Ready to bake.

Follow instructions on pg. 6 for maintaining your starter from this point on.

- -

Keep track of

FRIENDSHIP STARTER (pg.4)

______	Day 1	Mix ingredients.
______	Days 2-5	Leave alone.
______	Day 6	Stir one time. ______
______	Day 7	Feed. ______
______	Day 8	Stir one time. ______
______	Day 9	Stir one time. ______
______	Day 10	Feed. ______
		Ready to bake.

Follow instructions on pg. 6 for maintaining your starter from this point on.

CHART FROM

FRIENDSHIP BREADS, Starters and Recipes
P.O. Box 50053, Austin, Texas 78763

CHART FROM

FRIENDSHIP BREADS, Starters and Recipes
P.O. Box 50053, Austin, Texas 78763

Keep track of

F'SHIP YEAST STARTER (pg.5)

______	Day 1	Mix ingredients.	
______	Day 2	Stir one time.	_____
______	Day 3	Stir one time.	_____
______	Day 4	Stir one time.	_____
______	Day 5	Feed.	______
______	Day 6	Stir one time.	_____
______	Day 7	Stir one time.	_____
______	Day 8	Stir one time.	_____
______	Day 9	Stir one time.	_____
______	Day 10	Feed.	______

Ready to bake.

Follow instructions on pg. 6 for maintaining your starter from this point on.

Keep track of

F'SHIP YEAST STARTER (pg.5)

______	Day 1	Mix ingredients.	
______	Day 2	Stir one time.	_____
______	Day 3	Stir one time.	_____
______	Day 4	Stir one time.	_____
______	Day 5	Feed.	______
______	Day 6	Stir one time.	_____
______	Day 7	Stir one time.	_____
______	Day 8	Stir one time.	_____
______	Day 9	Stir one time.	_____
______	Day 10	Feed.	______

Ready to bake.

Follow instructions on pg. 6 for maintaining your starter from this point on.

CHART FROM

FRIENDSHIP BREADS, Starters and Recipes
P.O. Box 50053, Austin, Texas 78763

CHART FROM

FRIENDSHIP BREADS, Starters and Recipes
P.O. Box 50053, Austin, Texas 78763

Keep track of

FRUIT STARTER #1 (pg.18)

______	Day 1	Mix ingredients.	
______	Day 2	Stir one time.	_____
______	Day 3	Stir one time.	_____
______	Day 4	Stir one time.	_____
______	Day 5	Stir one time.	_____
______	Day 6	Stir one time.	_____
______	Day 7	Stir one time.	_____
______	Day 8	Stir one time.	_____
______	Day 9	Stir one time.	_____
______	Day 10	Stir. Add ingredients.	
______	Day 11	Stir one time.	_____
______	Day 12	Stir one time.	_____
______	Day 13	Stir one time.	_____
______	Day 14	Stir one time.	_____
______	Day 15	Stir one time.	_____
______	Day 16	Stir one time.	_____
______	Day 17	Stir one time.	_____
______	Day 18	Stir one time.	_____
______	Day 19	Stir one time.	_____
______	Day 20	Stir. Add ingredients.	
______	Day 21	Stir one time.	_____
______	Day 22	Stir one time.	_____
______	Day 23	Stir one time.	_____
______	Day 24	Stir one time.	_____
______	Day 25	Stir one time.	_____
______	Day 26	Stir one time.	_____
______	Day 27	Stir one time.	_____
______	Day 28	Stir one time.	_____
______	Day 29	Stir one time.	_____
______	Day 30	Ready to bake.	

CHART FROM

FRIENDSHIP BREADS, Starters and Recipes
P.O. Box 50053, Austin, Texas 78763

Keep track of

FRUIT STARTER #2 (pg. 20)

______	Day 1	Mix ingredients.	
______	Day 2	Nothing.	
______	Day 3	Nothing.	
______	Day 4	Stir one time.	_____
______	Day 5	Nothing.	
______	Day 6	Nothing.	
______	Day 7	Stir one time.	_____
______	Day 8	Nothing.	
______	Day 9	Nothing.	
______	Day 10	Stir one time.	_____
______	Day 11	Nothing.	
______	Day 12	Nothing.	
______	Day 13	Stir one time.	_____
______	Day 14	Nothing.	
______	Day 15	Nothing.	
______	Day 16	Stir one time.	_____
______	Day 17	Nothing.	
______	Day 18	Nothing.	
______	Day 19	Stir one time.	_____
______	Day 20	Nothing.	
______	Day 21	Ready to bake.	

CHART FROM

FRIENDSHIP BREADS, Starters and Recipes
P.O. Box 50053, Austin, Texas 78763